Mosslight

by
Kimberley Pittman-Schulz

કે

Winner of the 2011 FutureCycle Poetry Book Prize

FUTURECYCLE PRESS

www.futurecycle.org

Mosslight

Published by FutureCycle Press
Mineral Bluff, Georgia, U.S.A.

ISBN 978-0-9828612-9-5

for Terry

In memory of Merle & Judy
&
with gratitude to the animals in my life

≈

"Why did you stop praising?"
"Because I've never heard anything back."
"This longing you express is the return message."

—Rumi

≈

Contents

IV

V

Genesis

It all began with
an amoeba singing

against the fear
of separation

one throatless note
static

then the fluid soul
torn apart.

I

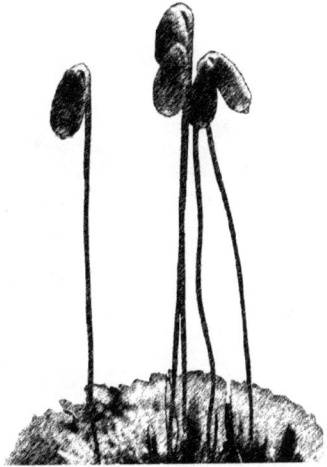

Kimberley Pittman-Schulz 9

10 **Mosslight**

Magic

When a bird dies, if you place the empty purse
of its body under the green velvet
of a catalpa leaf, nestle it
among berry canes and nettle,
the leaf will curl brittle, catch on a thorn,
scrape wind, earth-low, overlooked,
and where the bird was,
will be bent grass.

Once, when my mother bent to kiss
her three small girls, leaned into their breathings,
letting her lips tap theirs, the sound
reminded her of water dripping into other water,
but later, when the house stood scorched,
every window a black, gaping mouth,
where that sound had been,
now, one child.

These things could be magic
or physics or god.
No one really knows.

Box

With butcher knife, careful,
I cut two holes in a wall. Light
and shadows spill in. *Windows.*
They face away from eyes,
my mother's, but others' too.

I am seven, still bones
and a thin drape of muscle,
my cardboard room scented
with lilacs, aimed at the dogwood,
the shore of milky blossoms,
four petals, the center eye.

A long time drifting in grasses,
so many bees skimming past
and dragonflies, blue damselflies,
ordinary houseflies pausing to wash
their complicated faces.

Clouds gather grey, sore
with thunder. I whisper songs, my voice
more buzzing. Windows flash,
then the gravel of rain. Pinecones thud
to mud, *oh, like shot geese.*

Opening six jars, I dip my fingers.
No one is calling, so I sing
louder. One purple flower droops

into a blur of wings. *The bees in their furry coats*
must be wet. For curtains, yellow smears,
thumb prints of tempera paint.

Tracks

For every two steps, four paws pressed sand.
Last night a gibbous moon bit
through thin fog, the beach
luminous, so you'd have seen that dog,
that man, heading North alone,
their shadows together for miles.

The dog meandered, a loopy gait,
the man walked as if he had
some place to go. Look, here beside
the bleached stump—empty tin of tuna,
apple core taunted by bees—the pair rested,
smeared sand all that's left
of dreaming. I let my tracks fall beside theirs,
and if the tide doesn't swallow them,
whoever follows me will think,
a couple with a happy mutt.

The shore narrows until there is
only ocean and cliff face, then my solitary path,
returning, bearing new weight,
this mystery, these sea-smoothed stones
safe in my pockets. At least
he had a dog.

After Chemotherapy

I can do nothing but watch
a sky ripe with stars, spilling a path of light
over her bed, a brilliance fading
until there is one faint star
slowly receding, the last point of light
as the night turns itself off,
a dim face, a tiny white bird drifting away
into a universe so edgeless
and vacant it might get lost.

The mountain opens its red mouth
and red clouds fly out and crows oddly quiet,
just the panting of their wings
against the still air. Scattered on her floor
are a few pale pink and deep rosy flowers —
no, just the crumpled tissues
into which she coughed.

Soaking her wash cloth in steamy water,
I gently bathe her back, each vertebra
pushing up like a buried pebble,
then her shoulders hunched from years
of fine needlework, then her hands,
slender, with their unblemished olive skin
rippling over veins, her ruddy palms,
her long, perfect fingers that remember

doing all of this for me, then her feet.
I hold and separate each toe to swab
the web of skin in between. For the first time,
I see my mother.

Was it Christ or the Buddha who said
"make of yourself a light"? My mother
is a star, cooling. Each day her body,
with its heart of fire, consumes itself,
flinging out a little less light,
drawing us closer.

Seeds

All morning, a pocket full of seeds—
morning glories from Zimbabwe,
moon flowers from China, the cosmos
of Tanzania, Japanese trowel opening
this ground, and on the cedar bench,
chá preto, Brazilian black tea steaming.
This hill of mud and mulch holds
all my pretty pebbles hauled
from the mouth of the Mad River
and hours kneeling at Agate Beach,
the occasional fossil moved with me
from Pennsylvania, Washington, old oceans
turned stone, the impression of shells beside
shells of limpets and periwinkles
brought home from Fiji.
A global garden here.
The hands of strangers touched
each seed, so every blossom
will bear a sweetness, the unmet life
shadowing each interior. The tongues
of hummingbirds back from Mexico,
tongues thin as pins pricking deep,
will shine, a brief blur, licking.

Web

Giving water to the cannas, I saw it—
filament of light strung among
the huge fans of leaves—

an orb weaver,
fractures of orange and black shooting
over the humped back—

morsels of papery wings suspended with
last night's fog and silk-bound droplets of fly, beetle,
blown leaf litter all glittering.

Sorrow is never this light.
How tragic never to look up and see
whatever hangs shining before you.

When I tapped the longest strand,
she clambered down to investigate
on her marbled legs.

My eyes, each larger than her whole body,
must have seemed like caves. I felt
her peering deep inside.

Morning Prayer, Late July

I am brushing loose fur from this cat
and singing some dumb song to him.
Can you hear me? He's nearly twenty, kidneys starting
to fail, hips a bit arthritic. When the sun arrives,
I'll pinch spent blossoms from the hanging petunia
and trim the brown, crisp stalks from marigolds
and black-eyed susans. Thank you for the rain
that came in the night, slow and heavy,
like fruit falling again and again
through the forest's million leaves. Just now
two bats pedal their blackness above the pond,
and the sky, remembering that rosy light,
practices its pink version of morning.

I've been saving his white fur in a plastic bag,
with the tortoise-shell fur of his companion
gone since last November. I've been turning
old, dead flower heads, crumpled
leaves and stems into the garden soil.
As much as I can, in notebooks,
I've been keeping track of those bats,
the evening tree frogs, the various shimmering
snakes (even the ring-necked one, surprising in the kitchen),
the birds that come and go (we're not far
from junco season, you know), and the animal tracks
vague but visible on the trail (remember

the beetle tracks, delicate as embroidery
on a scrap of snow that one warm February?)—
all the little miracles, the surprising ways in which
the world keeps becoming one thing and then another.

I'm not sure what I am supposed to be
doing here. Lately there's been war
and cancer and children stolen
right out of their beds and the usual waning
of birdsong as autumn approaches,
and I can't figure out what to do about any of it.
Every day someone—a mother or father,
some finch or fox, a stand of spruce—dies,
but so far I haven't been among them.

So I'm just tending to what is here.
I've washed that teacup nearly every day
for more than a dozen years, swept squirrel scat
from the deck all summer, pulled strands
of my own hair, often grey, from my jacket
with a wad of tape. I let myself be happy
over nothing in particular—just now a woodchuck
picking an overripe banana and a cantaloupe rind
out of the compost pile, holding one
and then the other in his nappy, black fingers
as he eats. He watches me watching him
from the window while I bite a peach,
the two of us feeding the same body.

Storm

Rain splatters the window;
beyond, the young pine thrashed

and thrashing the wind. I wonder
when you will leave.

Restless, rooted in this
dirt, limbs held, go limp.

Below the pine, a halo
of needles, your glove half buried.

October

Winter wrens pick
among the white bones
of a fallen birch.

Everywhere the leaves are undressed,
their green coats gone, their naked
colors—reds, golds, ambers—exposed.

The eyes look longer each day
into the darkness—old fears, like stars,
hurling their history at me.

Three dawns in a row, a screech owl
mumbles from a sparse limb; then, as if
a dark ribbon, he flutters loose.

My Mother's Voice, Calling

I wake to the sound of my own name
shouted once into deep night—
or is it the bats returning early
to warm gaps in the roof's cedar shakes?

When finally clouded light crowds the window,
I find myself, standing in thrush song
that echoes upward, amid dragonflies stunned
on the cold tips of reeds, remembering
only the beauty of what I've lost—
how much easier it is
to love the dead than the living.

Air keeps slipping into my lungs
as if a tide rocking a shell. This breathing animal,
tired and flawed and afraid, still here
in the breaking wave of morning.

You do not need to be forgiven.
The clumsy heart, splashing in its
dark pool, arrhythmic and regretful, wants
these words to be true. The eyes,
glancing and darting, follow quick warblers,
their colors exciting the firs. *You do not
need to be forgiven.* I watch as they land in puddles
of last night's rain to bathe.

II

Flood

I thought: it's only brown water,
a hand, fluid, reaching to me.

No, it is bruised clouds, a hungry mountain,
the dying away of snow.

I wade the shallows—limbs
of trees float past and fur clotted
with leaves, debris, all swept away.

Balmy night, wet to thighs.
Then in deepening loss, a shoe
full of mud, rain, tiny fish.

Sleepless Heart

At first it is a kneading, a small animal, worried,
wanting out. You wake, palm to chest.

Bright fog beyond the windows,
and you recognize the moonlit interior, the gouged
and pockmarked stone, its quiet rhythm
through wet haze, caught, reflecting
some other beauty.

You remember being told: *The cells of the heart know only*
how to be a heart. It was a long time ago.
Now your body is a clutch of moss
grown around that knot of cells rioting,
that clump of red electricity
you hold but can't touch.

The moon, sinking, separates
shadows from mere blackness, drains
over the body of your calico stretched in sleep,
paws twitching, some dream of a chase,
then pummeling, suckling, a sigh, surrender.

It isn't darkness that you lie in
between night and morning.

Palm to chest, eyes shut, you try to go back,
to go in. The cells of the heart pulsed

before you could call them a heart, in the days
when you could have grown a tail, mitts for hands,
thumb of a head, dark purple panes of alien eyes,
that nub of brain aware of nothing.

Lewis River, Breathing

This morning, fog
in the firs. It drifts like a damp veil,
blotting out both ends
of our shallow canyon, the only world we see
is whatever lies immediately before us—

at the edge of the river, tracks
of possum and raccoon
among the dismembered bones
of a late steelhead, ribbons of fast grey water,
the irregular tempo of river surging
around half-sunken stones,
and the scent of spent salmon
coming on gusts of wind, pungent
then gone.

You can tell me how big and mean
the world is, but I can only point
to this one, here, now,
cradled in the yellow light
of the last alder leaves,
kinglets like high-pitched bells, dipping
their golden heads as if to listen,
the glistening of wrens and mosses
and a single ox-eye daisy, rising,
persistent, out of a thin frost.

This morning the world is small
and kind enough—see that amber leaf
angling to earth, its slow spiral?—
you can reach out or leave it
to the mud.

Oranges

Still raining. The maples, getting naked.
A fox sparrow, turning over fallen leaves
as if reading the scattered pages
of a book. And you? What are you doing now?
I am listening to pencil scraping paper,

wondering how thought, surges
of my body's own electricity,
the automatic flexing of muscles
and tendons, turn lead and blank sheet,
rain, tree, bird, leaf into what I mean

to say to you. Wax cools, one candle spent,
the flame of another pointing away
from my breath. I write: you are here
beside me; we are eating
wedges of orange, your fingers stained

slightly orange, your lips smelling of orange
as you lick the sticky juice
from your thumbs, making little
smacking sounds. If I write this,
isn't it true? A cup of tea

is seawater, a tide pool on the desk;
my calico curling in a box, the still eye

of a hurricane. You have a sliver of orange pulp
on your cheek. It will be a warm, sunny day.
I am always so happy.

December, Something Lit

Night. A loose bead of light
in the garden, bright, then dim,
bright again in the mulch,
a pulse. Another dark morning,
it's there on the deck, too.

The beam of a flashlight
finds a glowworm, a larva, homely
and gone dull in artificial glare,
consuming the golden gel, still as ice,
of a banana slug.

I don't know what illuminates
a glowworm, chemicals I've read,
but maybe it's only desire.

I'm at that time of life
where something is always flaring
or extinguishing.

I bring a fir into the house,
trunk cut and sappy, feed it tapwater,
twist silver and gold into its branches.
I've done this many times. Now so happy
to be doing it again. Now so happy
because I may not do it again.

There is light and hunger
all around us that we never see.

There is also the glistening path
slicking leaves, gumming ferns, up the trellis,
winding below the threshold we step through
each day, life proving itself
over and over. *I used to have antennae.*
I might have climbed that tree.

Mice and Shrews

Already this winter, I've buried
three deer mice and two short-tailed shrews
under snow, frozen leaves, once in the
briefly thawed surface of soil. I've tucked two
near the foundation of the house, planted one
in the stubble of the wildflower bed, laid two
at the edge of the forest, as if
returning them to their old lives.

I find them in the basement—
this one newly dead, the body tender
as an overripe peach, this one firm as a fist
in a suede glove. You're not supposed
to touch the dead, remember? Something
about germs: you can't see them,
but they're there. For years I confused death
with god and the wind.

But I want to touch, to hold each
mouse and shrew in my bare palm,
stroke the dense nap of brown fur
that is, I tell you, incredibly soft.

Look at the detail of fine mouse whiskers,
the bony feet barely covered by
a thin sheath of skin, the cord of a tail
that signs her presence in dirt, the way

light illuminates the red web of tiny veins
in each ear, delicate as a petal. See the shut eyes
of this shrew, the facial hairs fastidiously clean
and neatly combed, the pad at the tip
of his pointed nose, a bead of leather
able to drill tunnels in snow and part the earth.

Stunning that a mouse, a shrew,
can be so perfect and vacant—
but then I am reminded of butterflies
under glass, how butterflies fold their wings
when they die, and if you want to keep them
pinned and glued in flight, you must work
quickly, forcing their fragile wings wide
as lymph and life drain away. Tell me now,
what is this softness I hold in my hands?

Forsythia

There is just one cut branch
of forsythia, but in the chill
corner of muted north light,
it blooms for a month, a single strand
of yellow stars, a ladder of golden
petals for the eyes to climb,
a way out of winter
and this room.

Outside, rows of forsythia
stand naked and grey, their tangled limbs
full of knuckles. What is there
that doesn't ache for color
and a little more light? Look—
the cardinal is a brilliant red bud; the sun,
a deep orange cave; the mountain ridge,
a blur of blue loping horses in the distance.

When the forsythia finally open
their fists into flowers, they will smear
the sticky grains of longing onto
the chins of bees and the ruby throats
of small, swift birds. The old hedge will flame
with sex and humming. When you see this,
let it enter you. Every dull brain
needs to glisten with such yellow heat.

January

Juncos and grouse quilt the snow
with their walking, from the weed-stubbled edge
of the field to its center where they lifted.

Grey stones of a tumbled-down
foundation steam just barely
in the low angle of sunlight and cold air.

Our bodies beneath our clothes
are warm, like peaches in a brown bag,
sweetening in the heat of their own flesh.

Far from where it began, the earth turns
toward starshine every afternoon,
sending each day back home.

❧

It is right that somewhere
yellow flowers bloom
without me, their fountains of sugar
sipped away by insects, by quick green hummers
I'll never meet. Watching petals

of snow, I sit beside the fire
with an elderly cat, so still
it seems; but I know how we
spin together with every flake of pollen,
every crumpled wing, how the sun

consumes its own heart
so that we can float in constant light,
our eyes, even in deep night, open
like fissures trying to drink in
the last flash of day.

2 a.m.—Opossums

Possums are wandering
below open sky, six of them,
now seven, tumbling out of dripping ferns,
leaving crooked paths of laid-down grass,
nosing mosses, licking seeds,
bright, awkward bodies
in moonless light,
all glistening.

This night, for no apparent reason,
I wake—why? Here I am, standing
at the glass door, seeing all of this,
mouthing, *wonderful, wonderful.*

Orchids

On the telephone, my father speaking
of the way he slices steak
into strips, lays them together
with sweet yellow onions, slivers of
cheese, the precise way
he folds the flour tortilla to hold everything
together, then how he grows
tomatoes in the basement
under a bright lamp not far from the orchids
laden with buds, breaking
into blossom.

Later, awake in bed, I think of my father
three hours into the future,
folded into a quilt my mother made,
into the fragile veil of sleep that holds him
each night, the big house silent
except for the gurgling of baseboards
sputtering their heat and the hum
of those lamps in the basement, the air
still parted and moving where he stepped
from vine to vine, then the long look
into the open faces
of his flowers.

One March night, I am there.
He wakes briefly, propping himself up
on a shaky arm, and says, *I have to go
somewhere,* then he drops back,
a grey furrow in the white pillow,
and through the window, bare maples,
fractured moon, one winged seed
out of season, spinning and drifting.
At home, orchids turn toward light
in the greenhouse, their lavender petals
splotched and soft, their purple lips parted
as if about to speak.

Garden

The spent lupine
lays its purple petals,
its whole spine of blooming
down into the mulched soil
and becomes it.

There is someone
who watches
each papery petal drop,
knows the moment the stalk
simply gave up,
heard whatever soft crashing
the fallen beauty made.

❧

Yesterday, snow out of season.
It melts into the sinking mound
where we buried our dog, white ice
announcing his presence in the stone
where we carved his name,
all winter this sight; still,
it surprises me.

Somewhere a fir leans,
resting its back against wind and stars,
a Douglas fir I once knew, and now
this odd longing for that tree.

It leans and lets go, leans and
lets go, more than a century now,
never falling.

≈

Watching shrews
take moss into a new burrow
in the fern garden,
it occurs to me: I'll know
the mystery of their dark, earthen lives
someday.

I'll be part of that nest—
the moist, moved soil round
as peas, the niche
in the white lightning of roots
into which they drop
their babies
like secret plums.

Aubade

The moon, arriving late
and partial, is encircled by a ring
of thin clouds, as if one enormous cell
or atom suspended above the mountain,
chiding, *you are nothing more*
than this.

Dawn is far off,
so no one cares about this flock
of cedar waxwings passing
overhead, how their flight
has the sound of a hundred
quick exhalations. Who could know
that the high-pitched mewing
deep under ferns is shrews, or that
a rush of falling stars shows
its last fire to me?

I know that it is
neither because of me
nor for me that the world
keeps on going. Still, lavender light spills
at the horizon and stalks of milkweed
stand in silhouette, each shaking loose
its crop of monarchs
before it withers.

Woodbine gathers its green stars
around my feet, the first light slivering
the woods. I want to be in this breaking
day the way any bear would be, my body wiser
than words, my dark belly heavy
with blueberries, dew and webs
crusting my lips.

III

Kimberley Pittman-Schulz 49

Traveling

Yukay, Peru

You cannot get to that place
you see—the poor but happy child
wanting your coin, the church wall
with its layers of paint exposed, yellows
then green, the cracked plaster where
hands keep touching, the small room,
the uneven wooden chair knocking
at the floor as you sit, strand of curtain
disturbed by draft, your presence.

In the muddy fields, feet are clotted
with mud and ankles swollen
from long days of standing, leathered men
beside girls. On the path, donkeys,
the strange mix of indigenous skirt
and tee-shirt, two boys washing a parrot
in the aqueduct cut down from
the mountain five hundred years ago,
smiles, then eyes averted.

You walk the valley of partial walls,
chiseled stones, mortarless, all a blur
in afternoon sun, the room
you left, lost, scent of eucalyptus,
precise rows of potatoes and beans,

until you find the edge of town,
and there, dog eyes, staring,
a mongrel drinking in old rain,
now two.

Blue Morpho

Near the Madre de Dios River, Peru

Like a fragment of brown, marbled paper
or mottled bark flaked loose from a tree,
the butterfly went unnoticed on a leaf
until it propped open its wings, broad as
an outstretched hand, and let the filtered sun
flood into its million luminous blue scales.

Its wings, lifting the black velvet cord
of its body into flight, are openings
cut into this day. We can see that
god and death and all the angels
are brilliant, metallic blue
behind the heavy curtain of damp air,
the ordinary fabric of dusty yellow light.

Our souls must be small and fluid
to slip through such an elusive gap,
to enter the erratic flash in the foliage,
penetrate the quick spark
at the edge of the path.

At this moment, pure blue fire flutters
before us. We walk toward it,
happy and amazed.

The Urubamba River

Aguas Calientes, Peru

Fast, brown water was a long exhalation,
a persistent letting go in the lush foliage,
a chorus of rough voices beneath
our balcony, sighing a slow, repetitive *ah.*
When rain fell through the trees,
we heard its scattering and sizzling and applause,
bromeliads and orchids, taking the soft seeds
of warm water into their folds, receptive
as women in love or hungry birds.

Our room was a niche, a recess hollowed
by the Urubamba's constant sound and breath.
On the floor, red hand-made tiles were slick
with river sweat, and in a corner, a millipede
kept slipping down the whitewashed wall.
Doors wide open, we lay inside under
a thatched roof, deep in the canyon
of a single afternoon. Our mouths in dim light
were like trout bumping gently together
in a current—our hands, anemones brushing
the clay banks of our separate bodies,
making them flourish—our lungs, inhaling
the musky scents of river-laden air, moss swelling
in leaf shadow, and our own skin, damp and porous.

I don't know why, but every afternoon
like that must end. Now there is dishwater
and the clatter of glass, our days as familiar
as coffee grounds and egg shells on the counter,
waiting to be fed to the garden. Quick, reach across
the room and hold me now. I want to be
buoyant as a ripple of reflected sun
that purls and leaps and never spills.

After Darwin

Isabela Island, Galapagos, Ecuador

For years, kneeling, then long hours
spent watching—beetles and sheep,
hand bones, dog paws, wings of a cormorant
stretched black, in daylight, illuminated.

Even on a ship, all that ocean,
home a far hill below the water,
salt of spray, salt of sweat, salted meat
for supper, consumed and consuming.

Where he steps may well be moon
but for the finches, what flutters
at the ankles, ribs, overhead—variations.
Later the natives look familiar, almost kind.

Airport

This one seat, a fortress—
beyond it, tall sunlit windows
and strangers, the sudden jolt
of arms brushing, tiny hairs electric.

The caged cat moans but doesn't wake
the child bedded on linoleum, her cheek
on a man's shoe, a wingtip, the floor
shining under dirt, and warm.

Raven's Fire

Sitka, Alaska
for Barbara, the captain

The interval between lull and rise
guides her. She glides up swells, looking
for the next clear peak or white-crested wave.
When they come close together, she lets
the boat rest, the bow spooning up
spray and kelp. Among the marbled murrelets,
we are one more bird bathing itself
in salt water and sea thermals.

Long days like this, you don't want
the light to end—being small and vulnerable,
you want to feel your own margins.

Anchored in the calmness
of a cove, skimming out from the boat
in a kayak, you paddle very slowly
in the twilight between one day and another.
She says, *When you hear me moving in the wheelhouse,*
you'll know it is time to wake. You listen.
The sound of lips smacking all night
is water licking the hull.

The Cook

Raven's Fire
for Luda

Luda peels the skin
from pears, singing,
and makes them into bread.
She brings us each a slice
and we eat it, our bodies filling
with that sweet fruit—
pulp of pear and her bare voice
surprising as a stray seed
slipped from her tongue
to ours.

Simple

Chicagof Island, Alaska

Deer tracks fill with rain
and shiver. Some tiny insect flails
and spins, as if a divided hoof
creates new, great lakes
in black mud. High-up spruce needles
could be stars, a nearby deer fern
another universe, the bent face of a 'shy maiden'*
one far-away angel wondering
what to do.

Who says you're not some part of god?
When you lift the fleck from its crescent puddle
and put it on the soft shore
of sphagnum moss and watch it
skitter away, who says there is
no gratitude? Isn't the world larger
because you are in it? This could be what
your life was meant to do, this one gesture.
It could really be that simple.

*'Shy maiden' is the common name for a petite Tongass wildflower, the
blossom of which is bent toward the ground.

Grizzlies

Camp Denali

Three bears
in low red leaves.
Sow, two young.

There for no one,
not for you, nor me—
nose to ground, they graze.

Still, our eyes
take them in
and hold them,

each a wedge of light
with blonde fur, slight hump
at the neck that makes

our blood surge
as we watch them step
this way, see their heads lift,

each face paused
to look, to wait for scent
or sign on a gust of wind.

Our hearts fast
in our chests
say these bears are real,

which now drop their mouths
back down to nudge
spent blooms, then lick

the frost that mattes
thick fur at the root of
each arced claw.

Rogue River

Launching at Galice

Everywhere around us,
quaking—the grey-tipped fingers
of a submerged willow point up,
throbbing against the cool, green current;
foxtail grasses on the ridge we just descended
blur and quiver above the dry, thin steam
of hot stones; feathers of the fallen jay,
blood-glued to body, wave
on a useless hinge, empty wing beating
air and earth, air and earth. Above us,
one bald eagle circles twice then follows
a cloud into the trees that shutter
and sway. We are drifting
into the wild skin of an animal
amazing itself.

෨

Grave Creek

Mergansers with babies on their backs
join us at a distance, running the riffles
that spark with noon sun.

Reaching our first rapids, there is a gravel bar,
and we take the left channel. Across the scrubby island,
we see the three mergansers, their cargo

of small red bills chirping, all rising
and falling with the contour of earth, sand,
the stone basin beneath the river.

As we navigate, pivoting and lurching, they float,
lithe, swift, reaching the confluence before us.
While we prepare for a four-foot drop,

their rusty tails disappear into a clump
of equisetum around the bend. Left with our oars,
we are watched by eyes, ink-dark, protective.

&

After Kelsey Falls

There are no people
for a long time. On the banks,
black mud, splintered ribs of spent salmon,
parallel ruts left by deer drinking
from an eddy, harvest brodiaea
purple and fluted. Our raft lies like a body
on its back in the water. You sit among
the bones of its pelvis, your long
wooden oars, its arms, stroking the current.
Stretching out on its bloated edge,
I let my stomach absorb the heat
of its taut skin. Looking down into the river
where my face floats beside us—balls of granite,

serpentine, so many stones flying
below the surface of my eyes, cheeks, chin,
quick and colorful. They are like blood cells
rushing through the thin walls
of a vein; this moment, a being
we keep resurrecting.

ॐ

Huggins Canyon

The sky is strung like a purple tarp
atop the walls of granite and the tips of snags
more than a thousand feet up.

You stand beneath it, the low moon
at your side, both of you with partial faces
in the dim light of this deep river canyon.

Black water surges with sturgeon, slow and primal,
and a sudden splashing of otters emerging
to look at us, their faces wet, a dark luster, then gone.

I see one half of your mouth, speaking
of tomorrow's water and the take-out point
a half-day away, mice, voles, shuffling in brush.

As you squat to scrub a blackened salmon skin
from a pan, the moon stretches into night, washing away
the weaker stars, carving shadows into our tent.

Seen Things

Not a twig, but a tail,
grey-green in pebbles, yellow beneath,
the lizard off in poppies or ferns;

a husk of spider, black costume
perfect but empty, caught
with dew, threaded into web;

the young sea lion, biting ocean,
suckling air, washed in waves—
here her jawbone, scrap of leathered skin
among purple shells, hot sand;

light on petals, wet stones, oiled water
flicks color into my eyes
so I am a cave full of paintings,
every seen thing a splash of graffiti

when I shut out the light, lids down
over my own blue; it's all there,
and I can take the world with me.

Noche de los Muertos

The dead cope by licking
the insides of our ears.

We reach up with a finger as if to find
the cause of the sensation, but never do.

Feeling erotic, we turn to our lovers
and pull their skin into ours,

while the dead press their lung-less chests
into our summer screens, watching.

For an evening, the dead
are satisfied.

IV

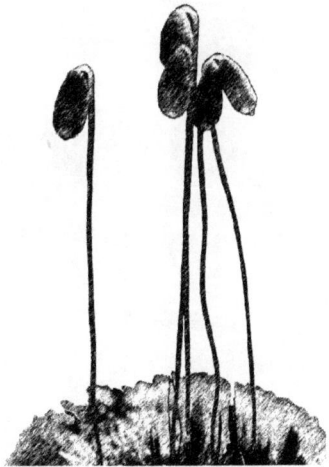

Tending Our Watershed

The daily surprise—waking
in river sound, the pulsing rush
through budding alders, weep
of cedar limbs, low reed grasses,
then mist rising, so much green
sighing at once.

How can I hold on
to these days? how can you?
this beauty persistent but disturbed.
With bent backs, we pull away
knapweed and foreign blackberry canes,
kill the knotweed, suffer the small injuries of thorn
and stinging nettle, until suddenly we stand,
stretching as one animal, glancing across
a landscape of wild bleeding hearts,
Nootka roses, trillium, the 'natives' among
the mounds we've made of roots,
stems, feral flowers wilting.

Later your fingers
find my bare shoulders,
drops of your blood like wild footprints
at my collarbone, your hands moving
from one beloved task
to another.

Today, the Mosses

Every morning there is the struggle
to focus on that one thing
that I will choose to love—

today, the mosses and the low-growing lycopods,
rising up with their tiny intricacies,
their piney branches, their trembling
at the movement of my feet.

Hyacinths draw out their swords,
slicing through that green felt
of late winter. If all sound could be heard,

the sun bearing down on those sharp blades
might tinkle like wind chimes, the mosses sighing,
the creeping ground cedars whispering,
look at me.

Getting Close

Suddenly a garter snake, the yellow ribbons
on her back, waving. I let her
ripple the shallow water, pulling me
into the pond. Then a robin, sighing
in a thicket, leads me into leaves—the coolness
of webs and unripened berries
brushing my forehead.

How close can you get
to a white oak, a tiny red velvet mite
in the moss? For how long
can you forget your separateness?

Who are you, anyway? Yesterday, eight rusty ants
dragging a dead wasp through the grass.
Today, one papery wing beaded with dew.

Suppertime, Early Spring

I step out into cold stars of snow
plummeting to earth. Their hearts are heavy
with a dim fire. They sputter their last heat
on my cheeks.

Inside, my husband brushes dirt
from mushrooms, severs stems
from caps. His face in the window
simmers with light. His back is a branch
bowed above his work, weighted with
concentration, those meadow mushrooms
filling his thoughts and our kitchen
with their pungent scent, their brown bodies
gorged on raw mud, dead grass, scat
of field mice, rotting bark, flooded shoots.

Out here the ground is softening
in places. Below my footsteps,
the dark plundering of last summer's insects
goes on, the silent limbs of crickets
scattering, the hard iridescence of beetle wings
dismantling, ants and spiders and true bugs
stewing, the soil ripening and blooming
with the first orange beads of tiny chanterelles.
On a maple stump, a yellow lace
of lichen sprawls, licking its own juices,

and a fungus, sweet with snow slush,
blossoms into what looks like
a thick, grey cabbage waiting on a table.

When I return home, the mushrooms
in the kitchen will be joined
with garlic, oregano, black pepper, pasta,
and the spice of my husband's skin.
Like two happy earthworms, we will
eat our daily portion of earth. The wet snow
will keep falling in small explosions
that settle down as clear yokes
of rain. We will dip our bread, drink wine.
With every bite, our mouths will be full.

June

The first morning glory
clenches its moon-blue petal
into a papery fist.

The white cat, old and aching,
lets his hips sleep
in a parcel of sun.

Our eyes open like seeds,
and something tender
reaches out.

Above, one swallow
keeps dropping
from a cloud.

Orchard

Sometimes the moonlight, pouring
brightly over the hill at dusk, wounds
the dangling fruit, that having
been exposed in its nightly riot
of sugar and worms, drops
to the ground.

By morning the moon
has moved on, the strayed
pear or apple gone, too. No one,
except perhaps a lucky raccoon,
notes its passage: how something simmered
with life only a few hours ago,
how one branch is lighter
and the grass, pressed flat and round,
is an empty dish.

Chrysanthemums

After weeks of drought that hugged us
in sweat and haze, wrenching leaves
from the woodbine, sending all
the new birds farther north—now,
at early September, residue of rain
and cool air. Pokeweed and spiders flourish
at shoulder's height, the blooming whiteness
of nettles and filaments of goldenrod
spraying their light at the edge of the woods.

Sometimes I am certain that I hear
nearby flowers opening, the small agonies
of sheaths torn open, the blossoms
emerging, every petal bright and important.

Then the long nights come. Your eyes
and mine read their own interior darkness,
scanning side to side, the eyelid—
a palimpsest. Below this moment's story,
another and another. Under those,
the one about void and miracle.

At noon you walk with grassy boots
into the kitchen, a spider in your hair,
hands full of chrysanthemums, each flower
a scarlet explosion wet with drizzle.
You put them in a clear blue vase
for me, filling it with water, promising me

that, when they are spent, you will
gather more. You say, *the mums*
will keep coming for a long time,
then you kiss me on each eye.

Hunger

Hunger is driving through the forests,
the wide open plains with their temples
of grass, the high mountain meadow
where the same pool of water
vacillates between snow and stream.
That empty space between nucleus
and orbiting electron, nucleus and cell wall,
is all craving. Look—here the leaf,
and now the leaf borer. Our skin in the linens,
and then the mites. Out in the garden,
a hornworm, his head in a tomato, feeds
a hundred tiny wasps bursting
from rows of white eggs on his back.
Always this one mouth. Every corner
has its spider collecting her juice and meat
right out of the air.

Every Morning

"Let the beauty we love be what we do."
—Rumi

This morning, as every morning,
our eyes rattle open, a crust of sand
in the corners, reminding us that every night
our bodies try to wander home
without us.

Don't rise and stand at the sink
combing hair, brushing teeth, thinking
of a thousand different details. Breathe in
the air of another new morning
and hum, filling the cavities of your cheeks,
the bone trumpet of your skull
with your own, reverberating music.

Let the terror of your
one and only face in the mirror
bless you and propel you.
Every globe of earth and ocean
is edged with light,
even ours.

River's Wind

for Terry

Late light on the river
shows us where the beaver lifts
his dark face
from darker water,
willow leaves in his lips, willow limbs
stripped and bare as bones
at our feet.

At the end of the day,
we feel the ending.
Two kingfishers rattle
in the firs and fall silent;
a single, yellow alder leaf
spins downstream,
sinking into dusk.

I look into your eyes
and see they are not pebbles.
The river moves in them—
both fixed and flowing, they are alive
in this moment, two blue flowers
caught in the river's wind.

The beaver drifts
toward us, just forehead and wet eyes
glinting on the surface, so that

in the dimness he could be
nothing more than water
folding in on itself.

A coolness lifts and
the sky bruises purple,
a dozen bats suddenly above us,
licking into the night. All we want
is here, now. I lean into your left arm,
each of us holding on
as long as we can.

What Beavers Know

Downstream is good
at the end of the day.

Rain on the willows
makes the sliver easier to swallow.

You can open a path through ferns—
just let your tail follow.

Eight years, maybe ten, if the forest holds,
you can take the river with you.

Returning

We can go back to that place,
let's believe in it, where ferns drip
and the little winter wrens drink then sing.
Our hands will be warm and clasped together,
our muscles, electric, our eyes as fast and blue
as the birds we try to follow into the sky.
Yes, there are the terrible wars
and the terrible words, but we won't let
what's been done and said
follow. It's morning. We can feel the cool fog
touch our skin and our skin touch back,
hear the quail cooing and shuffling
out of the woods, smell the chai tea,
taste the sweet jellied toast,
see a whole day, lush with time and choice,
still ahead of us.

∨

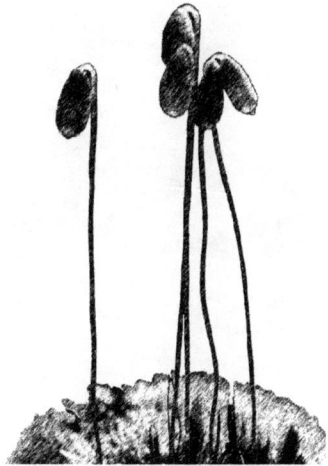

Kimberley Pittman-Schulz 87

Tide

Tide: Stresses exerted in a body by the gravitational action of another. . . . Every body in the universe raises tides, to some extent, on every other. —McGraw-Hill Encyclopedia of Science and Technology, 5th edition

Raven, is my mother
in there? I whisper.
Fog holds her to a limb,
beak, a black knife
held to morning's grey throat,
sky as indifferent
as it should be. Filigree
of poppy leaves breaks
the clay, earth opening,
a leaking sieve more than a gash,
a wound I keep wanting
to remember. Raven answers
with her wings, pumping wind,
then absence.

❧

Wild hare have left
their crumbling pearls
between dunes. Blonde sea grass
cuts and grabs, little pearl
of my own blood, sticky
then smeared with sand.

Kimberley Pittman-Schulz 89

Don't cry. How many times
did she say that?—catching
my tears in an empty Coke bottle,
showing me the wet stain
on a handkerchief. I stopped
crying then, so not to waste
some vital fluid we shared,
her cheeks streaked
almost daily. I wash the red crust
from my ankle, let in the sting
of saltwater. Fog purls up, veins of
purple clouds heavy on the horizon,
as the storm shivers then stalls,
holding back its rain.

&

Who can find that other place—
clouds torn into a blue field,
sun burning dew from orange petals,
the invisible life cleaning
delicate bone, hollow shaft
of feather, knot of hair? When someone
you love dies, for so long
you want to follow. Every month,
more than a year now, I've walked barefoot
on a flat, open beach, cold Pacific
pushing in, shallow rush of creek water

falling down, joining. Sometimes I count
dead birds, spread their mangled wings
into a still flight in sand. *No, not yet.*
A raven can live on air, and I can see
where this is all going. *No,*
not yet. Here. When I look back,
my footprints, crooked, weave the sea foam,
some places you might think
I walked into the tide
and it kept me.

At Risk

After the fire, they called the child
at-risk. What is that?
Somewhere sand slips down a cliff,
sanderlings run fast at the moving edge of water,
and that boundary where the earth stops
keeps getting closer.

I think of dipping a body full of salt
into salt water. I think
dissolving, also home.

Everything is water and particles, shifting.
Risk? Some people forget their next breath,
how we live by faith, knowing
that now will follow now.
Look at the sanderlings—there are
some that forage balanced on just one leg.

Moss Trail

Moss: my mind living outside,
reminding me that rain
is often a yellow-green fleece,

that river can be stacked in shadows.
Wet, under gibbous moon,
it is a glistening path, unworn threshold

through wooded edge. It licks at rock lip,
deer bones, the wind-fractured hemlock,
stark and lush, disparate ideas—

like my father, the sudden blue flash
of his eyes, here, also his dying
again, his waiting in the subtle burn

of those bleached sheets, seeing himself
looking down on himself, and being
an engineer, saying only, *how strange.*

Above me, wings collapse
out of first light into a crevice,
a mossy breach in the bark

of a decaying fir—all day
thinking of bats, thinking how safe
the darkness feels.

Wet, I Keep Talking

When another day begins in drizzle
and salmon sky, I tell you all that's wrong,
as if my need for you is a form
of resurrection. When the clouds
turn bright grey, the sun a deep muscle
pulling the day forward, I think *ashes*,
wish we'd opened the gaudy marble urns
before burying them. Both of you, stones
above the girls now 48 years deep
in roots. Your names, engraved,
hold mud. Rain leaks down
but can't touch you.

Nurse Log

Steam floats up from a prone body,
an old log, mossy and damp.

I go, lie beside it, whisper,
let's be organic together.

Out of the lichened wood, deer ferns
and the thumb of a coyote bush take root.

Fox scat in the shape of a cross
marks a passage.

There is a language larger
than words, the way breath rising

licks everything on its way up
and won't be contained.

A varied thrush thuds to ground,
his voice a wooden whistling.

Red mud stains robe hem,
rumpled cuff, exposed wrist bone,

palm to redwood corpse.
Quiet again—just this

scuttling of cool air through weeds,
my fingers flushed with touching.

Openings

This is what we are given:
soap and bees and dark tea,
coyotes calling on August nights,
milk and mist and the amazing nub
of a brown nipple that stands up
when it gets cold, the subtle smell
of earthworms tunneling soil, eating dirt.

This is enough,
and still there is more.

Today I saw the black face
of a dog lean out of a truck window
to sniff the air, his pink tongue flapping
in the wind, and I knew he could taste the sun,
the snowmelt, the early gnats and pollens,
his nostrils swelling with the cool silver scent
of car bumpers, grocery bags filled
with sweet yellow peppers and deep-red meat,
even the lushness of a single shoestring, mine,
dragged down ripe forest paths.

The dog seemed satisfied,
his body pure contentment
beyond gratitude—which, like grief,
doesn't last.

I don't know where that black-faced dog
is now. But the sun is smearing its white light
over us as it does every day, and tonight
the cold moon, as always, will turn
its blistered cheek toward us whether we see it
or not, and all of this is enough.

A Good Day

Dawn

The day lifts like a perfect body
pulled from water, dripping.

Tree frogs, red-legged frogs all
start singing.

The sound is a hundred hinges,
the body entering and entering.

~

Getting Clean

Both cats lap at my ankles as I step
from a shower, then they turn
to each other, licking and nipping.
The deer mouse hunted room to room
three nights running, sits preening
in the corner of my eye, tucked
behind a basket of books, tiny hands
scrubbing cheeks, crown, opaque ear.
Through the window, one sky, wild hair
of cirrus clouds washed with blue.

~

Morning Walk

The old fire trail,
walking, walking, walking;

redwoods leaning over both shoulders;
below each sole, millennia of crushed needles.

A hermit thrush scurries forward, pauses, tilting back
his head, opening throat, a gilded pink well,

ethereal music, as if the *birdness*
has flown out of the bird.

ॐ

Off to Work

Driving, immersed in jazz, this road
black tinsel through heavy leaves
of coltsfoot and spent trillium,
the landscape ridges and valleys. Suddenly
deep in a gulch the jazz breaks,
a baritone voice says, *consider only*
the best, the jazz just as suddenly back
topping a hill, the universe
momentarily un-encrypted. Driving,
no not god, but more than hawker.
I turn up the dial.

ॐ

On Campus

Three starlings, plumage flashing
copper, purple, oiled green in thin fog,
climb a ravaged trunk, talking like hawks
then trilling, looking into openings, yellow beaks
honeyed with cool emptiness.

I crouch to a poppy, a gaudy ornamental
among the native orange. Under my breath,
and mist slick, the blossom bursts. All morning
I walk halls, skim carpets, trousers cuffed
in red petals that won't let go.

&

A Meeting

Many voices at once, then calm. Cups lift
and each face sees itself tremble.

Beside me a woman talks intensely, her hands
tethered birds pulling into the air.

I focus on one thumbnail, a little arc of dirt.
What has that thumb been up to?

Cradling muddy shoots, scraping up shiny stones,
cleaning a dog's foot, the crevices between pads?

Her hands flutter and bank, that thumb
with its own crescent of dark moon.

Falling in love with those hands,
that thumb, their mysterious lives.

❧

Clam Beach, Pretending

Sanderlings wheel over damp sand,
legs a blur. As if pushed by wind,
they float North. Sparks fill their footsteps.
Godwits, whimbrels, sandpipers land
in an applause of wings, picking
at the glistening.

What if, in the next world,
we could be birds, more sanderlings,
trundling beside ocean on six toes,
black beaks stabbing shore, prying open
the wet edge, poking into the salt darkness
for some succulent morsel?

❧

At the Theatre, Kodo Drummers

Kodo, heartbeat. A room of battered skins
becomes something else.

My collarbone floats
in the sound of bees, a swarming,

the skinny bones in my chest
a ladder climbing down;

my body flushes, sweetness returning,
rhythm thick, pouring in, out.

≈

Late Night

Now a fox is yapping and whistling.
I feel his teeth grab my heart
soft as a shrew with her own teeth
chewing roots, hungry too. I've eaten moss,
breathed river, touched death, *it's so still*,
and I've seen how a single great-blue heron
is a form of light. The heavens have a saying,
but I don't know what it is. Awake,
and soon again sleep.

Autumn Evening with a Young Child

for Stephanie

A chipmunk stores seeds in his cheek
and, in the yard, a brown pear
sweetens the grass. Above us, clouds weave

into a single swath of linen
draped over the mountain, then the dim
rumbling valley. Everything is here—

the finches, the goldenrods, the last
pendulous leaves, the twin sounds
of our bodies breathing.

I ask, *where have the stars gone?* You look up
and say, *they are in the pockets of the sky.*
Clouds part briefly, showing us two flecks of light.

At Dusk, the Potato Vine

for Laura

Something comes, like scented air
filling an empty clay pot—breathing in,
something vague but familiar.
It is joy. It is that little red beetle
of bliss landed on your sleeve.
Afraid to disturb it, you sit still, awed,
trying to set every detail into memory
so you can command this moment
back out of your deep and restless life.

Nothing has changed.
Foxgloves still break into the mud
under their own weight. A certain
elderly woman folds her wide linens,
sobbing with grief. Friends carry
their cancers, gnawing inside them
like hungry grubs, from meeting
to meeting. Children stand barefoot
in the bush waiting for someone
to feed them. Planes land in the sea,
and whales strand themselves
on the shore. A scorched place
on the mountainside used to be a village.

Somewhere the sun rises
on a bruise, a stain of blood,
millions of hands, buried.

But here the potato vine vibrates
with the brightest green light
out of a corner, and you see it.
There is nothing more beautiful
than its heart-shaped leaves, its velvet
exuberant reaching, tumbling out
of its mossy basket, each tendril with its
tiny tongue of glossy new foliage.

For no reason, and not because you
are deserving, this gift—
this happiness so intense
that for a brief time you don't care
if you are the only one saved.

If I Could See the End Coming

I would wait for it. Where?
Beside the sumacs, under the beech
where the animals I've grieved
are a trellis of bones. I'd ask
the Carolina wren to spill out
her song. As the world condensed,
hyacinths, peonies, stargazing lilies
would bloom together, bathing everything
in their thick, sweet scents.

I wouldn't expect a sudden white light
or a familiar crowd on the horizon
waving me forward—just trees hiking
down the mountainside, winter creek
softening at the edges, filling with snowmelt,
tumbling toward me. My husband,
a river-runner, would be holding a trout
he carved from redwood burl, curved grain
giving momentum to fins, his voice
only in my head. *If you're swept away,*
point your feet downstream.

Beyond me, there'd be leaping,
the sporadic glimpse of deer, squirrels
threading understory. I'd nod
to a single black bear up on two legs,
the last wild man, savoring the air

above his face. I'd watch the low moon
step down from a locust branch, pause
at another, and slip away. All would be,
or seem, a slow process, like falling
in and out of love, again and again,
with the same person for years.

Walking Meditation

There is wet snow falling,
and I am in it, my own white body
like a spent star letting go of the sky,
drawn down to the mud of *here*,
the buds of *soon* and *almost*.

Most of the time there is no one
speaking my name, and I understand
how alone each foot burns
into cold layers, stillness pooling
around lopsided tracks.

I have already found inside
the little onion of dreaming, the way it roots
in darkness, sheds its skins
as it ripens inward, holding most tightly
to its own center, which is emptiness.

Listen, even in wet snow falling,
the wren sings, and wherever that singing goes
when he is finished—well, I'm pretty sure
that is the way home.

Acknowledgments

Grateful acknowledgments to the Pennsylvania Council on the Arts for a 2000 Fellowship in Poetry, the Concord Poetry Center's Colrain Manuscript Intensive program, and to the editors of the following magazines/periodicals in which certain poems first appeared, sometimes in earlier versions:

Avocet, "Blue Morpho," "Getting Close," "Mice and Shrews"

Cairn, "Autumn Evening with a Young Child"

The Northcoast Journal, "Returning," "Flood," "Tide," "Tracks"

The Oregonian, "Walking Meditation"

Rosebud, "Every Morning" (also selected for its 2000 William Stafford Poetry Prize)

The Merton Seasonal, "At Dusk, the Potato Vine" (also a finalist for the 2004 Thomas Merton Prize for Poetry of the Sacred)

The Sun, "Openings," "Morning Prayer, Late July"

Sow's Ear Poetry Review, "If I Could See the End Coming"

Toyon, "River's Wind," "Web," "Oranges," "Tending Our Watershed,""After Chemotherapy" ("After Chemotherapy" was also selected for the 2011 Jodi Stutz Memorial Poetry Prize)

Cover photo, "Moss Spore Capsules," by Alastair Thomson; author photo by Terry Schulz; cover design and typography by Diane Kistner; Palatino Linotype text with Candara Bold titling

The FutureCycle Poetry Book Prize

FutureCycle Press conducts an annual full-length poetry book competition open to any poet writing in the English language. The winning manuscript is published in both print and digital formats, with the poet receiving a $1,000 prize plus 25 copies of the published book. (Finalists may also be offered publishing contracts; those published are listed below.) Submissions of book manuscripts are accepted from January 1 to April 15 of each year for that year's competition. We also publish individual poems in *FutureCycle Poetry,* our online magazine. These poems, which remain online indefinitely, are collected into an annual print edition each November. All submissions must be received via our online submission form to be considered. To avoid unnecessary delays or unread returns, poets should review our guidelines at www.futurecycle.org.

FutureCycle Poetry Book Prize Winners
Mosslight by Kimberley Pittman-Schulz (2011)
Stealing Hymnals from the Choir by Timothy Martin (2010)
No Loneliness by Temple Cone (2009)

FutureCycle Poetry Book Prize Finalists
Leave It Behind by Emily Raabe (2011)
Castaway by Katherine Riegel (2010)
Simple Weight by Tania Runyan (2010)
Luminous Dream by Wally Swist (2010)
Beyond the Bones by Neil Carpathios (2009)